I0477988

Contents:

Introduction

I was inspired to write this book one time when I was listening to Grant Cardone on a YouTube video entitled, "Time is Money."

Grant Cardone is a successful entrepreneur who owns and operates several businesses and has real estate holdings worth around $350 million. He is the author of several books, including "The 10X Rule", "Sell or Be Sold", and "If You're Not First, You're Last". You can find out more of him on YouTube, Instagram, Google, and Twitter.

In his video he was talking about how he wrote a book called "The Millionaire Booklet" and sold 100,000 copies in the first month. The next day as I was outside doing my farm chores my thoughts wandered about that video and I was like, you know what? I think I'm going to write a book and sell hundreds, maybe even thousands of copies in a few months. I did further things with Caleb Maddix.

Caleb Maddix is a 16 year old who wrote his own book when he was 12 years old. He has earned over $300,000 and impacted hundreds of thousands of kids in the process. He is now the author of 9 books.

My goal is to be a millionaire by 20 years old and a billionaire by 40 years old.

About the Author

I am fourteen year old, Andrew Beiler. I live on a farm in Andover, New York. On my farm are cows, pigs, a horse and chickens. We make our own Maple Syrup as a hobby.

On the farm we sell Beef, Pork, Chicken, Eggs, Baked Goods, and Maple Syrup.

I love Bible Quizzing and sell meat sticks, pizzas and cookies to cover my expenses. Bible Quizzing is a great way to put God's Word into my heart!

Chapter 1   How Money Works

You probably bought this book because you want to know some of the things other people are learning on their journey to success. That is why I wrote this book; to show you some of the things I am learning on my first journey to success.

I am trying to find out how to earn money and how money works, and I want other people to come on the journey with me. This is what I already know.

You cannot make money. Making money is illegal. Making money is like taking a piece of iron and turning it into a real coin. You earn money, not make money.

Money is not just something that you can earn, spend like you want, and keep earning more money. Money is something that if you know its principles and apply them correctly, you can continuously earn more of it. If you don't know the principles you will keep having failure after failure and soon you will end up a broke person.

Don't do just anything with your money. You are going to spend too much money and end up broke like that. Have something to save up for and, until you have enough money to buy it, only spend a little or none of it. Don't spend all your money every time you earn some or you will never have enough money to buy whatever you are saving up for. Put your saved money somewhere safe.

Chapter 2   Setting Goals

Having something to save up for brings us to a very important step: Setting goals. First, let us define the term "goal". "A goal can be said to be "An aim or desired result." You might be thinking, "Well, do I have to know what my desired result is?" Yes, you do. Let me explain it this way.

Imagine you are watching a soccer game. There is one problem, though. There is no goal. The team lacks the desired result because the goal is their desired result and now there is none. The teams kick the ball around the field and do a few cool moves, but with no goal there really is no point to the game. I expect you would have stopped watching the soccer game after 15 minutes without having a goal to cheer for.

The same is with earning money. You can do a few cool things, but without a goal, life gets boring really fast. A goal makes anything a lot more interesting.

You don't know how to set a goal? The next few steps will help you set your goal.

Setting a Goal

Step 1: Find Your Passion

The way to set a goal is to find your passion. You will not succeed at something you do not like to do, so you might as well spend your time doing something you like to do.

Your passion can be absolutely anything, from playing video games, mowing lawns, and selling lemonade to writing short stories and operating big machines.

Anything you like to do, you can earn more money doing that than something that you don't like to do.

There are some stories of ways kids earned thousands of dollars by doing what their passion is, such as the above things.

Step 2: What do You Want to Accomplish?

What do you want to accomplish? (Accomplish: "Get done. Complete successfully"). Do you want to buy a luxury car? Do you want to become a governor? Anything you want to do, write it down. Your goal can even be to get good grades in school. Write it down. Let us assume your goal is to buy a luxury car, you can write it this way:

This is my goal:
I want to buy a luxury car.

Step 3: Get Clear

Now you have a goal, but it looks like nothing. That is why we have to get clear. Describe your goal. Say exactly what you want and how you want it instead of saying it with just one word.

This is my goal:
I want to buy a Black with a white stripe, "The King" Pagani

Huayra with black tires and black rims.

Step 4: Set a deadline

The last step of setting a goal is setting a deadline. A deadline is a time or date that you want to accomplish   your goal. You might think a deadline is not important, why can't I forget about a deadline and just accomplish my goal? You will never accomplish your goal that way. Let me tell you something.

Let us imagine that your school teacher gives you an assignment and there is no deadline for you to complete it.

14

You will probably not do the assignment. Or you may do a little now and then, but you never finish it.

Now let us imagine that your teacher gives you another assignment. The deadline is 2 weeks. You probably don't do anything until 13 days are past. Then you work really hard and get it done.

It is the same with life. Your goal doesn't have a deadline, so you never get it done. If your life goal has a deadline, don't wait until last minute but you will get it done. You are dead without a deadline.

Here is my goal again:

I want to buy a Black with 2 white stripes, Pagani Huayra with black tires and black rims by October 30, 2025.

I want you to stop reading and make your goal. Write it down and put it where you will see it every day.

Chapter 3   Accomplishing Goals

Now we have a goal, we just have to know how to accomplish it. (Accomplish: "Get done. Complete Successfully.")

Step 1: Putting Your Goals on Display

Once you have a goal, you need to have a way to constantly remind yourself about your goal. I think the easiest way is to find something that

17

connects with your goal and put it somewhere where you will see it every day.

For example, if you want to be a really good basketball player, you could hang up pictures of Michael Jordan, LeBron James, and Stephen Curry in your room. Every day when you walk into your room, you will see the pictures and they will motivate you by making you think about your goal. That will motivate you. I will talk about motivation in the next step.

Step 2: Motivation

The second step to accomplishing your goal is to

have motivation. (Motivation: "The reason or reasons one has for acting or behaving in a particular way.") If you followed the last step, whatever you did, that is like motivation. The reason you do something that connects with your goal is because you want to have that kind of success.

Another definition of motivation is: "Something that gives you energy to work toward your goal." Whenever I watch a success video on YouTube, I see something that someone else accomplished, or I get something done, I feel very powerful and confident. Then I work harder toward my big goal.

Step 3: Doing the Math

Doing the math is figuring out how much of what to sell to earn this much money. For example, if your goal is to earn $1,000, you could sell shirts at $10 apiece. That is where the math comes in. You would need to sell 100 shirts to earn $1,000. That may sound like it will take a long time, so make it simpler. Try to sell 5 shirts a day. It will take you only 3 weeks to earn $1,000. See what I mean? Doing the math makes everything seem easier.

Doing the math also works to make a huge goal simpler. Let us say your goal is to earn $100,000. That may seem huge and out of reach. Figure out how much of what to sell to earn $100,000. (You do not only have to sell things. You can also do jobs or errands for other people.) If you want to earn $100,000, I would advise you to sell or do a few things, such as writing a book and selling it for $10 a book. Work hard to sell them and you will have $100,000 in no time!

Parents, help your young kids write a book. Help them sell

it, and in a little over 4 years, they could have $100,000. If you think you can't write a book until you are about 20, I understand where you are coming from, but let me ask you a question; what is stopping your kids from writing a book right now? Is there any reason they have to wait until they are 20? There is none, right? Nothing is ever stopping you from taking action immediately except for your mindset. Caleb Maddix knows someone who is 7 years old and she has written 3 books.

"The gun that kills the most people is the gonna." A lot of

people say they are gonna do this, they are gonna do that, but they never actually do it. Instead, their dreams are killed by them saying gonna, gonna, gonna and by them never doing it. -Caleb Maddix

Step 4: Working For Your Goal

You advertised what you do, you hung up reminders, you have motivation, but all those are worthless if you do not do this one step. That step is: **Working for your goal**. This is a very important step to accomplish your goal, and for almost everything you do.

Having motivation and getting reminded does not get you money. It's the work you put into it that does. If you take a look at successful people, every one of them worked hard. None of them had overnight success. Therefore, know that **it takes hard work and patience to produce Success.**

Chapter 4   Earning Money

Now since we know about goals, we can finally get into earning money.

The first thing you have to know is: **Never give up.** When you start something, don't stop until it is finished. Before you start a project, make sure you have the time and resources, and you will finish it.

Don't write down your goals and think, the deadline is two weeks from now, I'll get started in 3 or 4 days. Start right now.

Starting with your goals right now is the second thing you need to know. Don't wait to write a book until you are 20 or 25 years old. Write a book right now. What do you want to be when you grow up? A millionaire, entrepreneur, dentist, astronaut? Start making money and becoming a millionaire or entrepreneur right now. Give speeches, write a book, and talk to millionaires and entrepreneurs.

If you want to be a dentist or astronaut, you will have to

wait until you are older, if you are a kid. But you can still watch dentist or astronaut videos, and intimate yourself with the training they do. You can talk to them and ask them to share their experiences with you. You can always do SOMETHING right now!

Chapter 5   Investing Money

The next step is to invest. Investing is simply spending money on something that will earn you a lot more money.

The first rule is: **Make sure you have a market for your product or service.** This is the rule that our family failed to apply the first few times we bought something for the purpose of making money.

What I mean by having a

"market" for it is making sure you have people that will buy enough of it so you can make profit.

This is the rule that most people fail to apply. They want to stock products or livestock like remote controlled vehicles or animals and resell them. Unfortunately, they don't have anyone to patronize them, so they have to sell it at cheap prices, make no profit and end up losing money.

That was what my brother Simeon, my dad, and I did. Simeon bought rabbits but he didn't have a market, and lost money. My dad and I bought pigs but didn't have a market, and lost money. We sold the pigs and rabbits at cheap prices.

The second rule is: **Make sure you will make profit and your customers will buy it at your price.** You now have a market but will you make profit at the price you are selling it? If you will, is it inexpensive enough for your customers?

We failed to do this too. We raise chickens and sell them. We used to feed our chickens NON GMO feed. (GMO stands for: "**G**enetically **M**odified **O**rganisms). That price is half ways between regular feed and organic feed. This plan wasn't the right one to attract organic customers and it was too expensive for frugal customers. We had to change the plan to partly GMO and part regular feed. We are actually getting more profit now that we dropped the price.

The last but not the least rule is: **Don't spend all your savings on an investment.** Even if you are positive that the investment will work, avoid emptying your life savings. ALL investments could fail. Every time you make an investment, make sure that if the investment fails or is slower than you expected, you still have enough money to keep going.

We also learned some lessons about this because it happened to us. We sold the pigs and rabbits and lost money but we still had enough money to buy something else.

Chapter 6: Putting God First

You should know how to earn money and you are going to impact people. But, don't forget this: No matter how much success you have, always put God first in everything. Remember this: "The one who has nothing on this earth and knows God is richer than the one who has everything on this earth but does not know God."

It is OK to be successful; it is OK to make a billion dollars.

33

That is great, but you have to remember God. "Money, success, and fame will die away, but God will last forever." In other words, don't set your heart on earthly things; they will go away sooner or later. Don't be so set on doing perishable things that you forget about the Imperishable One.

(Proverbs 16:3) Commit your work to the LORD, and your plans will be established.

This is just saying that if you devote your time to the Lord, he will fulfill your life goals if He sees it fit for you.

(Matthew 6:24) No one can serve two masters, for either he will hate the one and love the other, or he will be devoted to the one and despise the other. You cannot serve God and mammon.

This is not saying that you cannot be rich and have Christ at the same time. What this is saying is that you cannot devote your time to money and God at the same time. You can have money and God at the same time, but you cannot set your heart on both. Have fame but set your heart on God.

35

Chapter 7: Applying Information

Since you have read this book, you should know how to become successful. But even if you know how to become successful, it won't do any good if you only know how but don't do anything with the information you have. You will just stay the same, whether rich or poor.

This is the last but not in any way the least step in having success. In fact, this is the most important step in having success.

Information does not equal transformation, but information plus application equals transformation.

Finally, I want to tell you these three things. Whatever you decide to do, don't let it be P.O.O.R. (**P**assing **O**ver **O**pportunities **R**epeatedly). Make the most of your opportunities. Even when someone offers you a job that you don't like (it is your choice), if I were you, I would accept it because when your employer sees how good a worker you are, they might tell their friends, and new opportunities could come to you. You might even end up with a job you like.

Tell your friends about this book, and go earn some money. When you earn your first million dollars, make me the first person you contact.

Your friend and partner, Andrew Beiler

Email: bandrew23@yahoo.com

Facebook: Andrew Beiler

Twitter: @besuperinsane

Instagram: @think4millions